HIGHWAYS AND ROADS

Charlotte Taylor and
Arlene Bourgeois Molzahn

E Enslow Publishing

101 W. 23rd Street
Suite 240
New York, NY 10011
USA

enslow.com

Published in 2020 by Enslow Publishing, LLC.
101 W. 23rd Street, Suite 240, New York, NY 10011

Library of Congress Cataloging-in-Publication Data

Names: Taylor, Charlotte, author. | Molzahn, Arlene Bourgeois, author.
Title: Highways and roads / Charlotte Taylor and Arlene Bourgeois Molzahn.
Description: New York, NY : Enslow Publishing, 2020. | Series: Exploring infrastructure | Audience: Grades 3 to 6. | Includes bibliographical references and index.
Identifiers: LCCN 2018022672| ISBN 9781978503359 (library bound) | ISBN 9781978505094 (pbk.)
Subjects: LCSH: Roads—Juvenile literature. | Roads—History—Juvenile literature. | Roads—Design and construction—Juvenile literature. | Express highways—Juvenile literature. | CYAC: Roads. | Express highways.| LCGFT: Instructional and educational works.
Classification: LCC TE149 .T39 2019 | DDC 388.1—dc23
LC record available at https://lccn.loc.gov/2018022672

Printed in the United States of America

To Our Readers: We have done our best to make sure all website addresses in this book were active and appropriate when we went to press. However, the author and the publisher have no control over and assume no liability for the material available on those websites or on any websites they may link to. Any comments or suggestions can be sent by email to customerservice@enslow.com.

Portions of this book originally appeared in *Highways and Freeways*.

Photo Credits: Cover, p. 1 Blue Planet Studio/Shutterstock.com; cover, pp. 1, 3 (top) Panimoni/Shutterstock.com; p. 5 FPG/Archive Photos/Getty Images; p. 6 drmakkoy/ DigitalVision Vectors/Getty Images; p. 8 Andrey Bayda/Shutterstock.com; p. 11 Andrey Myagkov/Shutterstock.com; p. 13 Brian Maudsley/Shutterstock.com; p. 15 nicosann/ Shutterstock.com; p. 19 Bettmann/Getty Images; p. 20 Universal History Archive/ Universal Images Group/Getty Images; p. 23 Keep Smiling Photography/Shutterstock .com; p. 25 Kusska/Shutterstock.com; p. 26 Nicole S Glass/Shutterstock.com; p. 29 Vadim Ratnikov/Shutterstock.com; p. 32 CandyBox Images/Shutterstock.com; p. 35 Robert Asento/Shutterstock.com; p. 37 boyphare/Shutterstock.com; p. 40 Roman Samborskyi/Shutterstock.com; p. 43 Patrick Foto/Shutterstock.com.

CONTENTS

INTRODUCTION

Heading West on Route 66

"Get your kicks on Route 66!" These are the lyrics to a popular 1946 song written by Bobby Troup. The highway that is the subject of the song is one of the most famous and important in modern American history. Its own growth reflects the growth of the country. It also shows us that a road can be much more than a way to get from one place to another.

The Birth of Route 66

At the start of the 1900s, American roads were still in their early stages. There were more than two million rural roads, but most were not paved. They were also not all connected to each other. The country was growing fast at this time. The government knew that it was time to build bigger and better roads.

The Lincoln Highway opened in 1913. It stretched all the way from New York to California. That's a long highway! But there was a

Route 66 stretches out toward Albuquerque,
New Mexico, around 1940.

problem. Very few people had cars in the 1910s. Most of the people
who were driving the Lincoln Highway were wealthy. They were the
only ones who could afford an automobile.

In the 1920s, all of that changed. More and more cars were being
made. They became much more affordable. Soon, lots of people
had cars. And they wanted to hit the road. Again, there was a call to
build more highways.

Cyrus Avery and John Woodruff first came up with the idea to
build a route between Chicago and Los Angeles, two important

A map of Route 66 shows some of the main cities
along the highway from Illinois to California.

cities. The route was officially named Route 66 in 1926. In the early days, it was just a group of state and rural roads that were mostly in poor condition. It included lots of dirt roads.

The goal of the new highway was to connect the main streets in towns and cities all the way from Illinois to California. Building Route 66 meant taking a lot of roads that already existed and connecting them to each other. It took twelve years for all 2,400 miles (3,862 kilometers) of the highway to be paved.

Booming Businesses

Until this point, many of the towns and cities along Route 66 did not have major roads. But as time went on, the highway became more popular. Improvements were made.

Most business owners were thrilled to have a highway come to town. Highways brought people, and people would spend money. Lots of new businesses began popping up, especially gas stations, hotels, and restaurants.

The new highway wasn't just good for business owners. Farmers in the Midwest liked it, too. Being connected to other parts of the country meant they could move their goods, like produce and grain, faster and easier.

Truckers were fans of Route 66 as well. The highway was flatter than other roads and was easier to travel.

Road of Opportunity

In the 1930s, the Dust Bowl hit the middle of the United States. Massive dust storms destroyed crops and ruined many families. Hundreds of thousands of people left their homes and headed to California. Many of them took Route 66. For these people, the highway was their way to a new life.

When the Great Depression struck the country in the early 1930s, many people lost their jobs. The government wanted to get people working again. Route 66 provided a great opportunity. The government hired thousands of men to build and pave roads.

In the 1940s, during World War II, truckers used Route 66 to carry war supplies and materials to bases in the West. Once the war was over, many people, including soldiers, decided to relocate to California. Once again, Route 66 was the way to go.

As more and more people hit the roads, Route 66 continued to grow and develop. Smart business owners realized that all

Roy's Motel and Café in the Mojave Desert was a popular stop for drivers along Route 66 in California. It has even appeared in several movies.

travelers—not just wealthy ones—had to spend money. This was the start of affordable places like motels and diners. All along Route 66 these "mom and pop" businesses were thriving. Driving along Route 66 became an experience of its own.

End of the Road

By the 1950s, Route 66 was in bad shape. It was outdated. The two-lane highway was too narrow and could not handle all of the new cars and trucks on the road. Eventually, an interstate took the place of much of Route 66. The modern four-lane highway could handle a lot more cars and get them where they needed to go much faster. In the late 1970s, signs for Route 66 were taken down and soon the highway officially no longer existed.

Today, some maps include "Old" or "Historic" Route 66. Many spots on the route are listed in the National Register of Historic Places. People have realized what an important role the old highway played in the country's development. Route 66 affected all of the communities it ran through—it connected people and grew businesses. It also served as a bridge from the early days of dirt roads to today's modern interstate highway system.

Chapter 1

HIGHWAY HISTORY

The history of roads goes all the way back to the earliest humans. People who lived thousands of years ago needed food and water in order to survive. They had to walk to get to streams or rivers. They had to walk to find animals to hunt for food. They followed trails made by the animals. All of this walking created paths. As time passed, people gathered in areas that became villages and towns. The paths became well-used roads that connected these places. These early roads expanded once the wheel came into the picture.

The wheel was probably invented around 3500 BCE. It took some time, but someone figured out that the wheel could be used for transportation. Wheels were attached to carts, and then people could really move. They began to travel farther. With wagons, people could carry goods to different towns. Farmers and

People and animals walking from place to place helped to create paths that would later become roads.

merchants were able to trade goods. Soon people began to make their own roads. These roads were straighter and usually wider than the earliest paths.

Expanding Roads

Early rulers built roads for their soldiers and tax collectors. They needed to be able to reach all their land. Roads also made it easier for the soldiers to protect their country from its enemies. Roads were needed to help soldiers keep peace among the people.

Many rulers built short roads in areas of their countries. But rulers of China were the first to build roads around the entire country. The first of these roads were built to improve communication through-out the country. Postal stations were located along the roads. When a message had to get from one part of the country to another, a messenger would ride with it on his horse. He would be able to stop at a postal station for a new horse before moving on. This meant messages could get to their destination much faster than before. By the year 230, there were nearly 20,000 miles (32,187 km) of roads in the Chinese Empire.

The Silk Road

The most famous of China's ancient routes was the Silk Road. In fact, it was not just one road. It was an entire network of roads that ran through the country. The route officially opened in 130 BCE, when China's rulers decided to start trading with eastern Europe. The entire route stretched for 4,000 miles (6,437 km). It was named for the silk cloth that China produced. Chinese merchants would bring silk as well as tea, china, spices, perfumes, and rice to the Europeans. In exchange, they would receive animals like horses and dogs, honey, fruit, gold and silver, and even slaves. The Silk Road had a major impact on both China's and Europe's economy and culture. It lasted until 1453, when the ruling Chinese empire decided to end trade with the West.

This Roman road crosses the Gredos Mountains in Spain. It was built to carry armies and supplies and is still in good shape today.

Romans and Roads

The Romans were excellent builders of early roads. They began building them about twenty-five hundred years ago. Like the Chinese, the Romans depended on roads for trade. Also, the Romans ruled over a huge area, all the way from England to Africa. They often had to move soldiers over long distances. They needed good roads.

The Alaska Highway

In 1941, the Japanese bombed Pearl Harbor in Hawaii. It was the start of the war between the United States and Japan. In 1942, Japan attacked the American naval base in the Aleutian Islands of Alaska. Japanese troops captured two islands, Attu and Kiska.

The United States needed a highway between Alaska and the other forty-eight states. This highway would be a military supply route that would help protect Alaska. It would have to go through Canada. The government of Canada gave the United States the right to build the highway.

The United States Army Corps of Engineers built the highway. It was a big job! But the army engineers finished the highway in just eight months. It went from Dawson Creek, British Columbia, to Delta Junction, Alaska. Then the Richardson Highway connected Delta Junction to Fairbanks, Alaska. The road cost about $140 million.

In 1943, the United States recaptured the islands of Attu and Kiska. Soldiers and supplies could now be sent to Alaska using the new highway.

The famous northern lights can be seen along the Alaska Highway.

Roman roads were built on a solid base. The stone blocks they used were placed a little higher in the center of the road. When it rained, the water could run off easily. They also built ditches on the sides of their roads to carry the water away. Keeping the roads dry kept them from getting muddy and difficult to travel. The Romans built over 50,000 miles (80,467 km) of roads in their empire. Many of their roads are still being used today.

Log Roads

Corduroy roads were built as early as six thousand years ago. They were built in places where there were many trees. These roads were made by placing logs crosswise over the roadway. Corduroy roads were very bumpy. They were also very slippery and danger-ous when wet. There were many corduroy roads during the colonial days in America.

America on Wheels

The automobile brought about many changes in the roads. Earth, stone, or log roads were poor roads for cars. In 1908, the first con-crete highway in the United States was laid in Detroit, Michigan. The need for paved roads grew as more people began buying automo-biles. By 1924, the United States had over 31,000 miles (49,890 km) of concrete highways. The United States continued to build high-ways. Soon people could travel almost anywhere.

Chapter 2

BIGGER AND BETTER HIGHWAYS

The 1920s were a golden time in the United States as well as Europe. World War I was over. The economy was doing well. And Henry Ford's Model T changed the way Americans lived. For the first time, average people could afford a car. They were not just for the wealthy anymore. Americans loved the freedom of being able to drive. People began to hit the roads in large numbers.

Laying Out the Rules

As the numbers of drivers and roads increased, rules had to be made. One of the most basic rules was where to drive. In countries like the United States and Canada, cars must drive on the right side of the road. In places like Great Britain, Japan, and Australia, cars drive on the left side of the road.

Red, yellow, and green are the colors used for electric traffic lights. Red means stop, yellow means wait or get ready to stop, and green means go. The first traffic lights in the United States were put up in New York City in 1918. The first patent for a traffic light was given to Garrett A. Morgan in 1923. This traffic light had three positions. They were stop, go, and a position that made cars in all directions stop so people could walk. Soon traffic lights directed the movement of cars and trucks in all large cities in the United States.

Sometimes roads do not need traffic lights. Less traveled roads may have traffic signs instead. These signs tell drivers when to stop. The signs also tell drivers the speed limit—how fast they can go on the road. Some roads even have signs that tell drivers to watch out for animals, like deer.

Big Names in Roadways

Many people helped our roads and highways become what they are today. One of these people was Pierre Tresaguet, a French road engineer. In 1760, he came up with the idea of putting down layers of different size stones. Larger stones would be placed down first. Then a layer of smaller stones would be placed on top of that. When vehicles drove on the road, they would press down the layers of stones. This helped to form a strong and hard surface for the roads.

Henry Ford sits at the wheel of one of his Model T cars.
(Thomas Edison is seated behind Ford.)

Thomas Telford was a Scottish engineer who was known for building roads, bridges, and canals. In the early 1800s, he put a fine layer of small stones over his roads. Then he had heavy wheels roll over the surface to pack down the stones. This filled in the gaps and made the surface waterproof.

John McAdam was another Scottish engineer. He built on the ideas of people like Tresaguet and Telford. Unlike other engineers, though, he did not see the need for many layers of rock underneath a road. He believed the most important thing was a good road covering. In 1845, he was the first to seal road surfaces with tar. This made the roads smooth and dust free. It also made the roads last longer.

John McAdam created a new way to construct roads in the 1800s. Today, roads built with his technique are called "macadam."

In 1862, Colonel Pierpoint, an Englishman, built an island in the center of a street in Liverpool, England. Islands are still being built in the center of streets today. These islands help people to cross busy streets. Islands also separate cars going in opposite directions.

Changes to the Highway System

Soon many highways had been built. People did not always know which highway to take. In 1917, A. R. Hirst, from the Wisconsin

Highway Department, suggested that all highways should be numbered. In 1925, the United States began numbering highways.

Interstate highways run from state to state. Highways that travel east to west have even numbers. Highways going north to south have odd numbers. When this system was started, new maps were made showing the highways with their numbers. This made it much easier for people who did a lot of traveling. Today, all roads are named or numbered. Travelers can find the right road to take by looking at a map.

In 1956, Congress passed the Federal-Aid Highway Act. President Dwight D. Eisenhower signed the bill into law. It gave money from the United States

Henry Ford and the Model T

Henry Ford deserves a lot of credit for the improvement of roads in the early 1900s. He introduced the Model T in 1908. It was easy to drive. It was also cheap! The first one cost $825, which is equal to about $18,000 today. Ford used an assembly line that allowed his company to make lots of cars quickly. By 1914, his factories were making thousands of cars a week. Many people started driving cars. Narrow, dusty roads were not good enough for cars. New and wider roads with hard surfaces had to be built. More roads were needed because people wanted to travel to faraway places.

government to states for highway building. At first, $25 billion was set aside to build 41,000 miles (65,983 km) of roadways. States began building many new highways. Old highways were made better. Traveling throughout the United States became much easier.

Highway Features

As time went on, highways changed and improved. Driving was safer and more enjoyable thanks to features that were added over the years.

A highway that is built in a scenic area may have a turnoff called a scenic overlook. A scenic overlook lets travelers stop and look at the beautiful scenery without slowing the flow of traffic.

Signs along highways are also important for travelers. They tell them how far it is to the next city. Speed signs show how fast a vehicle can travel on the highway. Billboards are big advertising signs that tell about things a traveler can find in the next city. Some signs give numbers to call for emergencies or traffic updates.

Today, it is common to see electronic signs on major highways. These signs provide safety messages and warnings to drivers if there is construction or an accident ahead. They may even provide alerts in the case of a missing child in the area. These are known as AMBER Alerts, and they are a good way to get an important message to many people quickly.

Busy highways have rest stops. Rest areas have restrooms, water, vending machines, and sometimes picnic tables for travelers to use. Usually there is an information board with a map of the area.

Interstate highways carry a large number of
vehicles traveling from state to state.

Sometimes information and pictures about interesting things in the
area are also posted.

   In hilly or mountainous areas, highways have runaway truck
ramps. These ramps are very steep and have sandy surfaces. Big
trucks sometimes need help slowing down or stopping. The driver
can drive onto the ramp and safely stop the truck. Improvements
like these have made it safer and easier for drivers to use highways
and roads.

Chapter 3

STREETS AND SUPERHIGHWAYS: TYPES OF ROADWAYS

Imagine that you live in a small town. You set off in the car with your mom or dad to go to the mall in a nearby city. The road where you live does not have much traffic. There are no lines painted down the middle. It is a local road. These are the roads that connect your house to the rest of the community. They usually have low speed limits.

As you get to the edge of your town, you turn on to a busier street. It has four lanes of traffic. Cars and trucks are going much faster than on the local roads. There are a lot more vehicles around

Streets in neighborhoods are called local roads. Cars travel more slowly on roads than on highways.

you. You are now on a primary highway. These busy roadways connect larger cities.

Now let's say you live in a city. Your local road is called a street. Most city streets have two driving lanes in the center. They sometimes have a lane for parking on each side of the street. Whether you're in the city or out in the country, smaller roads with less traffic are called secondary roads.

Road Trip

Instead of going to the mall, suppose you are traveling to your grandparents' home two states away. You will probably take a freeway to get there. Freeways, or superhighways, are another kind of highway. Vehicles can enter or exit a freeway only at certain places called interchanges. Ramps are built at interchanges for vehicles to get off or on the highway. Interchanges have overpasses and underpasses. These are built over and under the

A toll plaza with E-Z Pass lanes. Electronic toll collection keeps traffic moving and allows drivers to pass through tolls without cash.

highway. Overpasses are also built over railroad tracks so that traffic does not have to stop for trains.

All freeways are not really free. On some freeways, travelers are charged money, called a toll, for use of the highway. These freeways are called toll roads. The toll money is used to help pay for maintaining the freeways.

What's that Road Made of?

Roads can have many different kinds of surfaces. Roads that have very little traffic have gravel surfaces. These roads wind through areas where very few people live. Vehicles cannot go very fast on these roads. Sometimes these roads are called rustic roads.

High-Tech Tolls

Tolls are not a new invention. People have been paying to use roads since at least the seventh century BCE. Early tribes would charge travelers who wanted to cross a mountain or river. The Romans often made people pay to cross bridges or enter city gates.

Today, toll money is usually used to help maintain and repair highways as well as build new ones. Until recently, drivers needed to pay these tolls with cash. In the 1980s, electronic toll collection was introduced. With this system, vehicles passing through a toll area can pay electronically through an account that has been set up. Electronic toll collection has several benefits. Drivers no longer need to carry cash. It saves money by lowering the number of toll collectors needed. It also keeps the flow of traffic moving since vehicles do not need to stop at the toll booth. In some states, vehicles can continue at full speed through the toll plaza. The E-Z Pass system is the largest electronic toll collection system in the United States.

Roads with heavy traffic need hard surfaces. Chemicals and tar are mixed with small stones to make asphalt. Road builders use asphalt to surface many roads. Trucks bring hot asphalt to a paving machine. The paving machine spreads the hot mix on the roadbed. Large rollers smooth the asphalt. The asphalt cools quickly. In a few hours, people can drive on the road. These asphalt-paved roads are sometimes called blacktop roads.

Years ago, asphalt for roads cost a lot of money. Today scientists have found a way to recycle the asphalt surface from old road-beds. A machine removes the asphalt from the road and grinds it up. Fresh asphalt is then mixed with the old ground-up asphalt. A paving machine then puts the asphalt mixture back on the road sur-face. Next, huge power rollers pack down the asphalt. This makes the old road like new. Soon it is smooth and ready for vehicles to travel on.

Major highways, such as freeways and primary highways, have surfaces of concrete. Concrete is a mixture of cement, sand, water, and gravel. Concrete is best when it is used for busy highways. It lasts the longest of any road surface. Concrete highways have fewer potholes and need fewer repairs than asphalt roads. Concrete sur-faces reflect light, which makes it easier for drivers to see when driving at night. Concrete is also the most expensive material for paving road surfaces.

A construction worker helps put down asphalt on a new road.

Road Obstacles

Road builders like to build roads that are straight and level. But sometimes obstacles get in the way of a straight road. When a road runs into a mountain, it may be difficult to build the road over it. Sometimes tunnels have to be built. This way, the road can continue right through the mountain.

Rivers are another obstacle to a road. Sometimes tunnels are built under rivers. There are also many types of bridges that let people cross rivers, railroad tracks, and other roads. All of them let people have the freedom to travel.

Chapter 4

WHO WORKS ON HIGHWAYS?

Building and maintaining a new highway is a huge job. A lot of planning must happen before the first bit of dirt is overturned on a new highway. After that, there are many stages of designing, constructing, fixing, and maintaining roadways. Let's take a look at the different jobs and careers in highways and roads.

Getting Ready

Planners are the first people needed when a new highway is proposed. They set up electric counters on existing highways to see how much traffic there is. Crowded highways can be very dangerous. If the counters show that the highway is too busy, a new highway may be needed. Planners also need to look at the effect a new highway may have on the environment. Highways should not harm important habitats. Planners need to look at how much air, water,

Surveyors stand near a highway as they make measurements of the area.

and noise pollution might be created by a highway. Once all of this is researched, planners have to find money for the roadway. Usually, this means that they must prove to lawmakers that tax money is needed for the road.

After these planning stages, surveyors and engineers begin to work. Surveyors use special tools to measure an area. They help to find the best place to put the new highway. Then the land is bought.

Engineers are usually in charge of building roads. They oversee everything from the planning to the design to the actual construction. Engineers have set standards for roads. They want to make sure that roads are safe.

Getting to Work

Sometimes trees or bushes are in the path of the new highway. Large machines are put to work to clear the land. They must cut down the trees. Sometimes buildings must be moved or torn down. Big trucks are needed to haul all these things away. Next come backhoes and bulldozers. These huge machines can dig large amounts of dirt at once. They level hills and move big rocks. People who have experience driving and working machines and trucks are always needed when highways are being built.

Workers are needed to make the machines that are used in road building. Workers are also needed to drive these machines.

The Big Dig

Boston's "Big Dig" was a huge road and tunnel project. The plan was to reroute the city's main highway to a tunnel. Engineers hoped that the new route would cut down on the city's heavy traffic. Beside moving the roadway, the project included a new bridge, tunnel, and park. It ended up being the most expensive highway project in the United States. Problems occurred at almost every step. There were leaks, design mistakes, and delays. There was even one death, when a ceiling collapsed in the new tunnel and killed a person in a car. The Big Dig was supposed to be completed in 1998 and cost $2.8 billion. Instead, it was done in 2006 and cost about $15 billion. It was an example of the challenges that engineers and workers face when taking on a huge project.

Mechanics are needed to keep the machines in good working order. They are also needed when a machine breaks down.

Dump trucks bring gravel for the roadbed. The road graders move the gravel in a certain way. The roadbed must be smooth and a little higher in the center. Then rain will run off the highway quickly. Heavy rollers are used to pack the gravel down.

Next, a movable concrete plant is set up at a halfway point along the highway to be paved. Large dump trucks are filled with wet concrete. The concrete is hauled to the paving machine. Steel rods are placed along the edge of the roadway. The concrete is dumped in front of the paving machine as it slowly moves along. The machine spreads the concrete evenly on the highway. As it moves, it places the

A worker operates a steam roller on a new road.

steel rods where the joints in the highway will be made. The steel rods make the highway stronger. The new highway is sprayed with a chemical to help the concrete harden.

Final Touches

Grass needs to be planted on the sides of the highway. Sometimes workers need to plant trees and shrubs, too. This helps keep the noise of the traffic from bothering nearby houses.

Depending on the kind of chemicals that are added to the concrete, it could take from several hours to several days for the new highway to harden. Once that is complete, workers need to paint lines on the road or highway. These lines divide the roadway into traffic lanes.

Many signs are needed on our roads and highways. They are used to show the locations of exits, distances to cities, and speed limits. Sign companies hire people to make these signs. After the highway is finished, police officers are needed to patrol the new highway. This means that cities and states might need to hire more police officers.

Maintaining Roads

Highways and roads need to be kept in good condition so that they are safe for all drivers. Litter has to be picked up. Holes and cracks must be filled. After years of wear and tear, most

A construction worker uses a spray machine
to paint white lines on a new street.

highways need to be resurfaced. In many places, winter storms bring ice and snow. Snowplows are needed to remove the snow. Salt and sand are spread on the roads and highways to help melt the ice. People must work all year long to keep roads and highways in good driving condition. Building highways and keeping them in good shape provides jobs for thousands of people.

Chapter 5

THE FUTURE OF HIGHWAYS: SAFETY AND TECHNOLOGY

People have lots of choices when it comes to traveling. They can go by plane, train, or boat. But many travelers feel that the best way to see the country is by car or motor home. Cars offer a freedom that other forms of transportation do not. Highways are an important part of the driving experience.

Besides offering the pleasure and freedom of travel, highways have another benefit: money. City officials want to have superhighways leading to their city. Good highways bring many people who spend a lot of money. This is good for business, and it helps a city

Traveling by car gives people the freedom to
go wherever they want at any time.

to grow. People also travel for business. There will always be a need for good highways.

The need for trucking gets larger each year. This means more large semitrucks will be traveling on our highways. These highways need to be able to carry the weight of these vehicles. More and better highways are going to be needed.

More superhighways are being built. These highways are mostly four or more lanes. They are divided highways. Cars on one section of the highway all go in one direction. On the other section of the highway, the cars travel in the opposite direction. Superhighways are made to go as straight as possible. Most of the sharp curves are cut out, and steep hills are cut down. Tunnels are made to go through hills and mountains. Also, new and wider bridges are being built.

Solar Roads

One exciting new aspect of road technology is the solar panel. These panels replace the asphalt surface and can be driven on by cars. They use the energy of the sun to create power. That power can then be used by local homes and businesses, power streetlights, and provide energy for electric car-charging stations. The panels can even provide heat to melt snow and ice on the roadway. The downside to solar panels? The cost. Even with the savings in electricity, 1 mile (1.6 km) of a solar roadway costs millions of dollars to build. Engineers are working on finding more affordable ways to use solar panels on roads.

Going Electric

Future highways may depend on the types of cars that we will be driving. Today, we have electric-powered or hybrid (electric- and gas-powered) cars. Until recently, electric cars could not go very fast. They were also very expensive. They needed their batteries recharged very often. These things are all changing. The newest cars can travel more miles on one charge. Some new models can go faster than gas-powered cars. And the price of hybrid cars is coming down. If electric cars become the norm, more charging stations will be needed on the roads. These vehicles may change the types of highways we have in the future.

Looking Ahead

In the future, buses and trains may become a more popular way to travel. People are becoming more aware of the car's impact on the environment. Mass transportation, like trains, is friendlier to the environment. If more people do choose this type of transportation, it would cut down on the number of cars and trucks on the highways.

Future highways might have more and better lighting. This will help make traveling safer. More and better noise barriers will be built. These barriers will protect the people living near noisy highways.

The highways of tomorrow may look different than the ones today thanks to new technology and changes in the vehicles that we drive.

Scientists are trying to find new ways to remove snow and ice from highways. This is important for people who travel in winter in places where it snows. Scientists hope to find chemicals that will cause less damage to both road surfaces and to vehicles. Some of the chemicals used today cause vehicles to rust.

Highways will always be important in countries where many vehicles are used. Highways let us travel to many different places, whether for business or for pleasure.

CHRONOLOGY

450 BCE Romans begin building roads throughout their empire.

230 CE Nearly 20,000 miles (32,187 km) of roads are built in China.

1760 Several layers of gravel are used to harden the surface of roads.

1845 Road surfaces are sealed with tar.

1908 One of the first concrete highways is laid.

1916 The United States government helps states pay for highway building.

1918 The first traffic lights are used to direct the flow of traffic in New York City.

1923 Garrett A. Morgan is granted a patent for a traffic signal.

1925 Highways in the United States are numbered to help travelers.

1938 Building begins on the first turnpike in the United States.

1950 Great efforts are made to improve highways in the United States.

1956 The Federal-Aid Highway Act is passed to help states pay for road building.

1985 Route 66 is officially removed from the US highway system.

1987 E-Z Pass, an electronic toll collection system, is founded.

2016 The US Interstate Highway System reaches a total length of 48,191 miles (77,556 km).

GLOSSARY

asphalt A dark-colored material obtained from oil; when mixed with sand it is used to surface roads.

backhoe A tractor-like machine, with a bucket at the end of a long arm, that is used for digging.

bulldozer A tractor with a blade that looks like a large shovel on the front.

concrete A mixture of cement, sand, water, and gravel.

contractor A person who agrees to do a job for a certain price.

engineer A person who studied in special schools and who knows a lot about how to plan and build things.

equipment Supplies and things that are needed.

mechanic A worker who keeps machines in good working condition and who fixes machines that have broken down.

patent A document showing that a person or group owns the rights to an invention.

recycle To use something over again.

rural Having to do with the country.

superhighway A highways that has four or more lanes going in one direction.

surveyor A person who measures land and can draw a map of the area.

FURTHER READING

Books

Allen, Benton, Paige Earl, and Trent Kelly. *How to Be an Engineer.* New York, NY: DK, 2018.

Burgan, Michael. *Who Was Henry Ford?* New York, NY: Penguin, 2014.

Doeden, Matt. *Spacex and Tesla Motors Engineer Elon Musk.* Minneapolis, MN: Lerner, 2015.

Websites

Build a Model Plank Road

www.sos.state.mi.us/history/museum/kidstuff/settling/build.html
Have fun making your own plank road out of craft sticks from this Michigan Historical Center website.

Historic Alaska Highway: A Road Building Epic

www.northeasternbc.com/historic.html
Find out more on the Alaska Highway.

Historic California US Highways

gbcnet.com/ushighways
Learn about some historic highways.

INDEX